Aston Vil Quiz Book

101 Questions To Test Your Knowledge Of This Prestigious Club

Published by Glowworm Press
7 Nuffield Way
Abingdon OX14 1RL

By Chris Carpenter
with additional contributions from S J L Cooper

Aston Villa Football Club

This book contains one hundred and one informative and entertaining trivia questions with multiple-choice answers. With 101 questions, some easy, some challenging, this book will test your knowledge and memory of Aston Villa Football Club's long and successful history. The book is packed with information and is a must-have for all loyal Villa fans.

You will be asked many fun and interesting questions on a wide range of topics associated with the Villa for you to test yourself. You will be quizzed on players, legends, managers, opponents, transfer deals, trophies, records, honours, fixtures, songs and much more, guaranteeing you both an educational experience and hours of fun. Educational, enjoyable and fun, this Villa Quiz Book will provide the ultimate in entertainment for Aston Villa FC fans of all ages, and will test your knowledge of Aston Villa Football Club and prove you know your Villa trivia in this fun addictive quiz book.

2019/20 Season Edition

FOREWORD

When I was asked to write a foreword to this book I was flattered.

I have known the author Chris Carpenter for many years and his knowledge of facts and figures is phenomenal.

His love for football and his skill in writing quiz books make him the ideal man to pay homage to my great love Aston Villa Football Club.

This book came about as a result of a challenge in a Lebanese restaurant of all places!

I do hope you enjoy the book.

Lloyd Cooper
Trinity Road Season Ticket Holder of many years

Let's start with some relatively easy questions.

1. When were Aston Villa founded?
    A. 1874 ✓
    B. 1884
    C. 1894

2. What is Aston Villa's nickname?
    A. The Aston Army
    B. The Claret and Blues
    C. The Villans ✓

3. Where does Aston Villa play their home games?
    A. Molineux
    B. St. Andrews
    C. Villa Park ✓

4. What is the stadium's capacity?
    A. 41,826
    B. 42,682
    C. 43,268 ✓

5. Who or what is the club mascot?
    A. Aston the Villan
    B. Bella the Lion ✓
    C. Hercules the Lion

6. Who has made the most appearances for the club in total?
    A. Charlie Aitken
    B. Gareth Barry
    C. Gordon Cowans ✓

7. Who has made the most *league* appearances for the club?
   A. Joe Bache
   B. Charlie Aitken ✓
   C. Nigel Spink

8. Who is the club's record goal scorer?
   A. John Devey
   B. Harry Hampton
   C. Billy Walker

9. What song do the players run out to?
   A. Escape ✓
   B. Mr Blue Sky
   C. Shoot the Runner

10. Which of these is a well-known pub near the ground?
    A. The Golden Lion
    B. The Holte Pub ✓
    C. The Villain's Escape

OK, so here are the answers to the first ten questions. If you get eight or more right, you are doing very well so far, but the questions will get harder.

A1. Aston Villa was founded way back in 1874, and was one of the original founder members of the Football League in 1897.. The club was formed by members of the cricket team attached to the Aston Villa Wesleyan Methodist Chapel who wanted to establish a winter activity.

A2. The club are known around the world as The Villans, and rightly so, as they are the seventh most successful team in English football in terms of honours won.

A3. The iconic Villa Park is where the Villa plays their home games, and it has seen many famous fixtures down the year, including many FA Cup Semi-Finals.

A4. Villa Park holds a capacity crowd of 42,682 with the home fans always in fine voice.

A5. Aston Villa has two mascots, so give yourself a bonus point if you knew that. Hercules and Bella goof around before home games, and they make a great couple.

A6. Scottish left back Charlie Aitken holds the Aston Villa appearance record. Aitken made 657 appearances in a 17 year career at Villa Park.

A7. It's that man again, Charlie Aitken. He made 559 league appearances for Villa, more than his closest rival's total club appearances (including cup games). He was a true loyal servant of the club.

A8. Billy Walker played for the Villans between the World Wars and scored a club record 244 goals during his 14 year stint with the club.

A9. The Villa players emerge from the tunnel to the spine-tingling strains of Escape by Craig Armstrong, raising the temperature inside Villa Park.

A10. The Holte Pub is located just yards away from the famous Holte End, and has been a popular drinking hole of choice for home fans for over 100 years.

OK, back to the questions.

11. What is the highest number of goals that Aston Villa has scored in a league season?
    A. 108
    B. 118 ✓
    C. 128

12. What is the fewest number of goals that Aston Villa has conceded in a league season?
    A. 30
    B. 32 ✓
    C. 34

13. Who has scored the most penalties for the club?
    A. Gareth Barry ✓
    B. Dion Dublin
    C. Steve Staunton

14. Who is the fastest ever goal scorer for the club?
    A. Juan Pablo Angel
    B. John Carew ✓
    C. Dwight Yorke

15. What is the home end of the ground known as?
    A. The City End
    B. The Holte End ✓
    C. The Witton End

16. What is the club's record attendance?
    A. 56,588
    B. 66,588
    C. 76,588 ✓

17. Where is Aston Villa's training ground?
    A. Bodymoor Heath ✓
    B. Cradley Heath
    C. Washwood Heath

18.   What is the name of the road the ground is on?
    A. Birchfield Road
    B. Trinity Road ✓
    C. Witton Lane ✓

19. Which stand has the biggest capacity?
    A. The Doug Ellis Stand
    B. The North Stand
    C. The Trinity Road Stand ✓

20.   What is the size of the pitch?
    A. 110x70 yards
    B. 112x74 yards
    C. 115x72 yards ✓

Here are the answers to this block of questions.

A11. Aston Villa's highest scoring season was a special one. In the 1930/31 season, the club scored an incredible 128 goals in just 42 games, an average of more than 3 goals per game.

A12. Villa has had some mean defensive campaigns in their time as well. In the 1971/72 season they only conceded 32 goals in 46 games. Pretty stingy.

A13. Long-serving midfielder Gareth Barry is Aston Villa's leading penalty scorer. He scored 18 out of the 23 he took for the club.

A14. On the 30th September 1995, Dwight Yorke scored against local rivals Coventry City just 13 seconds after kick-off. What a way to start a game.

A15. One of the most awe-inspiring pieces of architecture in football stadia, the Holte End is where the Villa faithful congregate on match days.

A16. The club's record attendance is 76,588. That many fans crammed into Villa Park to witness an FA Cup 6th round tie against Derby County on 2nd March 1946. This was in the days before all-seater stadiums and I doubt this record will ever be beaten.

A17. Villa hone their skills at the training base at Bodymoor Heath near Tamworth. The facility underwent major renovations in 2006 and is now one of the best in the country.

A18. Villa Park is situated on Trinity Road in the Aston area of Birmingham. It is a local landmark which can be seen clearly by motorists passing into Birmingham on the City Expressway.

A19. The newest stand at Villa Park is also the biggest. The Trinity Road Stand holds 12,954 fans on match days and also boasts many corporate boxes.

A20. The playing surface at Villa Park is 115 yards long by 72 yards wide and has provided plenty of room for the wingers and overlapping full backs over the years.

Now we move onto some questions about the club's records.

21. What is the club's record win in any competition?
    A. 10-0
    B. 11-1
    C. 12-2

22. Who did they beat?
    A. Accrington Stanley
    B. Everton
    C. Notts County

23. In which season?
    A. 1891/92
    B. 1901/02
    C. 1911/12

24. What is the club's record win in the Premier League?
    A. 6-0
    B. 7-1
    C. 8-2

25. Who did they beat?
    A. West Ham United
    B. Wimbledon
    C. Wolverhampton Wanderers

26. In which season?
    A. 1994/95
    B. 1995/96

C. 1996/97

27.   What is the club's record defeat?
A. 0-8
B. 1-8
C. 2-8

28.   Who against?
A. Arsenal
B. Chelsea
C. Tottenham Hotspur

29.   Who has scored the most hat tricks
for Aston Villa in the Premier League era?
A. Gabriel Agbonlahor
B. Christian Benteke
C. Dean Saunders

30.   How many senior England
international fixtures have been played at
Villa Park?
A. 14
B. 15
C. 16

Here are the answers to the last set of questions.

A21. Aston Villa's long history has included some pretty big wins, but none bigger than their record victory of 12-2.

A22. Fellow long-time members of the Football League Accrington Stanley were the opposition put to the sword on this record occasion.

A23. This game occurred over 120 years ago, in the 1891/92 season, so hopefully it doesn't give the Accrington fans too many sleepless nights.

A24. The Villains record victory of the Premier League era thus far was a 7-1 demolition.

A25. This record victory was at the expense of the Crazy Gang of Wimbledon, who will have been far from pleased to be on the end of such a beating.

A26. It's over twenty years since Villa achieved this record-breaking win. It happened on 11th February 1995, so it was in the 1994/95 season, and yet it still lives in the memory of many Villa fans.

A27. Aston Villa's record defeat is much fresher in the memory, which will be a cause of pain for many die-hard fans reading this book. This game happened as recently as December 2012, in the 2012/13 season.

A28. This 8-0 drubbing occurred at Chelsea. The Villa obviously picked the wrong day to play one of the most fearsome teams of the modern era. Villa keeper Brad Guzan actually played well; it was just that Chelsea were unstoppable on the day. Even Torres scored.

A29. The answer to this question is... All three! They have all scored one Premier League hat trick for Villa, and so have Tommy Johnson, Savo Milosevic, Dwight Yorke, Dion Dublin, Luke Moore and John Carew!

A30. Villa Park has played host to 16 England matches between 1899 and 2005, making it the first ground in England to have international football in three different centuries.

Now we move onto questions about the club's trophies.

31. When did the club win their first League title?
    A. 1894
    B. 1904
    C. 1914

32. When did the club win their first FA Cup?
    A. 1877
    B. 1887
    C. 1897

33. Who did they beat in the final?
    A. Birmingham City
    B. West Bromwich Albion
    C. Wolverhampton Wanderers

34. What was the score?
    A. 1-0
    B. 2-0
    C. 2-1

35. How many times have Aston Villa won the League?
    A. 7
    B. 8
    C. 9

36. How many times have Aston Villa won the FA Cup?

A. 6
B. 7
C. 8

37.   How many times Aston Villa won the
League Cup?
    A. 5
    B. 6
    C. 7

38.   Who was the last captain to lift the
League trophy?
    A. Gordon Cowans
    B. Dennis Mortimer
    C. Peter Withe

39.   Who was the last captain to lift the
FA Cup?
    A. Stan Crowther
    B. Johnny Dixon
    C. Les Smith

40.   Who was the last captain to lift the
League Cup?
    A. Ugo Ehiogu
    B. Gareth Southgate
    C. Andy Townsend

Here are the answers to this block of questions.

A31. The Villains captured their first league championship 120 years ago, winning the First Division in 1894.

A32. Aston Villa secured their first ever FA Cup 7 years earlier, lifting the most famous trophy in the world in 1887.

A33. This first FA cup triumph came against local rivals West Bromwich Albion.

A34. The game finished 2-0 to the Villa, and took place at the Kennington Oval in London on 2n April 1887.

A35. Aston Villa has won the top division of English football seven times in total.

A36. Aston Villa has won the FA Cup on seven occasions.

A37. The men in claret and blue have won the League Cup five times.

A38. Dennis Mortimer was the last Villa captain to gets his hands on the League trophy at the end of the 1980/81 season. He was once described as the 'best player never to play for England'.

A39. Johnny Dixon, who spent his entire professional career with Aston Villa, was the captain at the time of Villa's last FA Cup triumph in 1957. Villa beat Manchester United 2-1 at Wembley Stadium on 4th May 1957, and it really is worth tracking down the footage on YouTube, in particular to see Peter McParland score with a diving header.

A40. Now an analyst of some repute, Andy Townsend was also a pretty decent footballer, and was man of the match and captain of the Villa side that last won the League Cup when Villa beat Leeds United 3-0 on 24th March 1996.

I hope you're having fun, and getting most of the answers right.

41. What is the record transfer fee paid?
    A. £20 million
    B. £22 million
    C. £25 million

42. Who was the record transfer fee paid for?
    A. Darren Bent
    B. Tyrone Mings
    C. Wesley Moraes

43. What is the record transfer fee received?
    A. £24 million
    B. £28 million
    C. £32 million

44. Who was the record transfer fee received for?
    A. Christian Benteke
    B. James Milner
    C. Ashley Young

45. Who was the first Aston Villa player to play for England?
    A. Arthur Brown
    B. Howard Vaughton
    C. Both

46. Who has won the most international caps whilst an Aston Villa player?
   A. Gareth Southgate
   B. Steve Staunton
   C. Andy Townsend

47. Who has scored the most international goals whilst an Aston Villa player?
   A. Juan Pablo Angel
   B. Savo Milosevic
   C. Peter McParland

48. Who is the youngest player ever to represent the club?
   A. Jimmy Brown
   B. Gary Gardner
   C. Jack Grealish

49. Who is the youngest ever goalscorer?
   A. Leandro Bacuna
   B. Gareth Barry
   C. Luke Moore

50. Who is the oldest player ever to represent the club?
   A. Brad Friedel
   B. Jimmy Rimmer
   C. Nigel Spink

Here are the answers to this block of questions.

A41. Aston Villa's record purchase of a player currently stands at £22 million.

A42. This money was spent on Wesley Moraes who came from Club Brugge in June 2019. The initial fee for Tyrone Mings was £20 million, but it may rise to £25 million, if certain contract terms are met.

A43. The club received a staggering £32.5 million for one of their players in July 2015.

A44. Christian Benteke holds that record having been sold to Liverpool for £32.5million in 2015, surpassing the previous record of £26 million that Manchester City paid for James Milner.

A45. Arthur Brown and Howard Vaughton made their England debuts in the same match, against Ireland in 1882. The forwards scored 9 goals between them in a 13-0 victory for England.

A46. Ireland defender Steve Staunton earned 64 of his 102 caps for his country during two spells with Aston Villa. He was a great servant for both club and country.

A47. Northern Ireland striker Peter McParland is Villa's top international marksman, with 10 goals whilst at the club, including 5 at the 1958 World Cup in Sweden.

A48. Jimmy Brown played his first game for Aston Villa at the tender age of 15 years and 349 days in a match against Bolton Wanderers on 17th September1969. He went on to play for the club 75 times.

A49. Gareth Barry is the Villains youngest goal scorer. He netted in the Premier League aged just 18 years and 60 days.

A50. Of these three goalkeepers, American Brad Friedel is the oldest of all, and when he appeared in his last game for Aston Villa on 1st February 2011 against Manchester United he was a staggering 40 years and 4 days old.

I hope you're learning some new facts about the Villa.

51. Who is Aston Villa's oldest ever goal scorer?
    A. Paul McGrath
    B. Cyrille Regis
    C. Peter Schmeichel

52. Who is the club's longest serving manager of all time?
    A. Gerard Houllier
    B. Brian Little
    C. George Ramsay

53. Who is the club's longest serving post war manager?
    A. John Gregory
    B. Ron Saunders
    C. Graham Taylor

54. Who is Aston Villa's most-capped England player?
    A. Emile Heskey
    B. David Platt
    C. Gareth Southgate

55. How many Aston Villa players were in England's World Cup winning squad of 1966?
    A. 0
    B. 1
    C. 2

56.   Which of these is a fanzine?
        A. B6 Tales
        B. Heroes And Villains
        C. Up The Villa

57.   What animal is on the club crest?
        A. A Dragon
        B. A Lion
        C. A Tiger

58.   What is the club's motto?
        A. Prepared
        B. Preposterous
        C. Prosperous

59.   Who is considered as Aston Villa's
    main rivals?
        A. Birmingham City
        B. West Bromwich Albion
        C. Wolverhampton Wanderers

60.   What could be regarded as the club's
    most well known song?
        A. Hi Ho Silver Lining
        B. Holte Enders in the Sky
        C. Shine On You Crazy Diamond

Here are the answers to this block of questions.

A51. This is not a mistake. Peter Schmeichel really is Aston Villa's oldest scorer! He netted in the Premier League against Everton at Goodison Park on 20th October 2001 aged 37 years and 337 days.

A52. Villa's first manager is also their longest serving. George Ramsay was at the helm for an incredible 42 years, winning a hatful of trophies in this time.

A53. Ron Saunders was at the helm for eight years in the 1970s and 1980s and he was in charge of 353 games in that time. Villa lifted the League Championship and two League Cups during his time as manager.

A54. Former Villa centre back Gareth Southgate won 42 caps while playing for Villa.

A55. For a club that has produced so many England internationals, incredibly there were no Villa players in the England squad that won the World Cup in 1966.

A56. Heroes And Villains is the most popular Villa fanzine, and has been in circulation since 1989. It now has a very popular fans website which discusses all things Villa related.

A57. The famous badge of Aston Villa shows a rampant golden lion on a claret background. It is one of the oldest and most well-known club crests in the world.

A58. Aston Villa's club motto is simply "Prepared."

A59. One of the oldest and bitterest footballing rivalries in the world, the games between Villa and local rivals Birmingham City are often fiery affairs.

A60. Holte Enders in the Sky (to the tune of Ghost Riders in the Sky) is the most famous Aston Villa song.

Let's give you some easier questions.

61. What is the traditional colour of the home shirt?
    A. Black and White
    B. Claret and Blue
    C. Yellow and Green

62.   What is the traditional colour of the away shirt?
    A. Green
    B. Red
    C. White

63.   Who is the current club sponsor?
    A. Better Bet
    B. Unibet
    C. W88

64.   Who was the club's first shirt sponsor?
    A. Davenports
    B. Direct Line
    C. Dominos

65.   Which of these airlines have once sponsored the club?
    A. BMI Baby
    B. Thomas Cook
    C. Virgin Atlantic

66.   Who is currently the club chairman?
    A. Xia Jiantong

B. Randy Lerner
C. Nassef Sawiris

67.   Who started the 2019/20 season as manager?
A. Steve Bruce
B. Remi Garde
C. Dean Smith

68.   Who was the club's first black player?
A. Curtis Davies
B. Stan Horne
C. Dwight Yorke

69.   Who was the club's first match in the league against?
A. Watford
B. Wolverhampton Wanderers
C. Wycombe Wanderers

70.   Who was the supporters' player of the year for the 2018/19 season?
A. James Chester
B. Jack Grealish
C. John McGinn

Here are the answers to this block of questions.

A61. The only excuse for getting this question wrong is if you are colour-blind. The answer is, of course, claret and blue.

A62. Traditionally Aston Villa's away kit has been predominantly white.

A63. The current shirt sponsor is Asian online gambling operator W88. Villa has had a lot of betting companies as sponsors on a short term basis over the last few years.

A64. West Midlands brewery Davenports were the first company to sponsor Aston Villa, when the TV licensing rules were relaxed in 1982.

A65. To this day, no airline has sponsored Aston Villa. Maybe this could change if they can get back into Europe and rack up some air miles.

A66. Egyptian businessman Nassef Sawiris is the current chairman of Aston Villa.

A67. Dean Smith started the 2019/20 season as manager. He was appointed to the role in October 2018.

A68. Midfielder Stan Horne was Villa's first ever black player. He made his debut for Aston Villa in 1963, and was one of the first black players in

England. He only played for Villa 6 times, but he still made history.

A69. Black Country rivals Wolverhampton Wanderers were Villa's first ever opponents in the league. The match took place on the 8th of September 1888 and the game ended 1-1.

A70. John McGinn deservedly won the 2018/19 player of the season award.

How are we doing so far? Good? Let's get back to happier times.

71. In what year did Aston Villa win the European Cup?
   A. 1980
   B. 1981
   C. 1982

72. Who did Aston Villa beat in the final?
   A. Bayern Munich
   B. Juventus
   C. Real Madrid

73. Who scored the winning goal?
   A. Gordon Cowans
   B. Gary Shaw
   C. Peter Withe

74. Where was the match played?
   A. Amsterdam
   B. The Hague
   C. Rotterdam

75. Who was the manager when Aston Villa won the European Cup?
   A. Ron Atkinson
   B. Tony Barton
   C. Ron Saunders

76. Who was the captain who lifted the trophy?

A. Des Bremner
B. Allan Evans
C. Dennis Mortimer

77. How many of the starting eleven were from the UK?
A. 5
B. 8
C. 11

78. Where did Aston Villa finish in the league the year they won the European Cup?
A. First
B. Fifth
C. Twelfth

79. Which former Aston Villa player captained his country at two World Cup Finals?
A. Olof Mellberg
B. Martin Laursen
C. Alan Hutton

80. Which Aston Villa player has made the most appearances at World Cup Finals?
A. David Platt
B. Paul McGrath
C. Steve Staunton

Here are the answers to this block of questions.

A71. Aston Villa conquered Europe in 1982.

A72. Aston Villa defeated Bayern Munich in the 1982 European Cup Final. The match was an incredibly tense affair and finished 1-0 to the Villains.

A73. The name of Peter Withe will be passed down amongst Villa fans for the rest of time. He became an instant club legend by netting the winner against Bayern with his goal in the 67th minute.

A74. The match was played on 26th May 1982 at the Feyenoord Stadium in Rotterdam.

A75. The manager of the European Cup winning side of 1982 was Tony Barton. Ron Saunders had the honour of winning the league for Villa the season before to ensure they qualified for the European Cup. This was in the days when only those who had won their league entered the competition, unlike the Champions League of today where you can finish fourth in the league and qualify.

A76. Dennis Mortimer lifted the European Cup that glorious evening. He was some player, and a very good captain.

A77. All of the eleven players who played in the 1982 European Cup Final were from the UK. Eight were English and 3 were Scottish. How times have changed.

A78. The season that Villa won the European Cup, they finished twelfth in the First Division. It was all about priorities that season.

A79. Swedish defender Olof Mellberg captured the hearts of the Villa faithful in his time at the club, and also captained his country in two World Cups. A true great.

A80. Nicknamed "God" by the Villa fans, Irish defender Paul McGrath has played in 9 World Cup Finals matches, more than any other Aston Villa player.

It's time to crank up the difficulty. Are you ready for the next set of questions?

81. What is the official Aston Villa website address?
    A. astonvilla.com
    B. avfc.co.uk
    C. villa.co.uk

82. Who is Aston Villa's top scorer in the Premier League era?
    A. Gabriel Agbonlahor
    B. Gareth Barry
    C. Dwight Yorke

83. What is Aston Villa's highest home attendance in the Premier League?
    A. 44,347
    B. 45,347
    C. 46,347

84. Who has made the most Premier League appearances for Aston Villa?
    A. Gabriel Agbonlahor
    B. Gareth Barry
    C. Alan Wright

85. Who is the oldest outfield player to play for Aston Villa in the Premier League?
    A. Gordon Cowans
    B. Paul McGrath
    C. Robert Pires

86. Aston Villa against whom is the most played fixture in English football?
   A. Birmingham City
   B. Preston North End
   C. Everton

87. Which ex manager was the first from outside the UK to manage in the top flight?
   A. Gerard Houllier
   B. Paul Lambert
   C. Josef Venglos

88. Which Aston Villa player scored the first ever goal at the Emirates Stadium in London?
   A. Martin Laursen
   B. Olof Mellberg
   C. Zat Knight

89. When did Aston Villa last play in European competition?
   A. 2007/08
   B. 2008/09
   C. 2009/10

90. Who did they lose to in their last European match?
   A. CSKA Moscow
   B. Lokomotiv Moscow
   C. Spartak Moscow

Here are the answers to this block of questions.

A81. avfc.co.uk is the address for the official website.

A82. Local boy Gabby Agbonlahor is the club's highest scorer in the Premier League, with 73 goals in total, 13 more than Dwight Yorke.

A83. The record Premier League attendance is 45,347 for a match on 7th May 1994 against Liverpool.

A84. Former England midfielder Gareth Barry made 365 appearances for Aston Villa in the Premier League, almost 100 more than his closest rival Agbonlahor.

A85. Arsenal legend Robert Pires played for Villa in the twilight of his career, and was 37 years and 182 days old at the time of his last appearance for the club.

A86. Aston Villa versus Everton has happened no fewer than 217 times down the years, as both of these founding members of the league have been almost ever-present in the top flight.

A87. Born in modern day Slovakia, Josef Venglos was the first foreign manager in the top flight of English football. He was appointed manager in the summer of 1990, but only lasted a season as Villa finished only 2 places above the drop-zone.

A88. Towering Swedish centre back Olof Mellberg scored the first ever goal at the Emirates Stadium, meaning he will go down in history not just in the archives of Aston Villa, but Arsenal too.

A89. Aston Villa's last venture into Europe came in the 2008/09 season when they made it through a tricky group and into the last 32 in the UEFA Cup (now the Europa League).

A90. For reasons that escaped us then, and still do, the manager at the time, Martin O'Neill chose to field a weakened side in the away leg, including two debutants, as Villa were defeated 2-0 in Moscow to lose 3-1 on aggregate.

OK, we made it. The final set of questions is upon us. Here we go.

91. Which Aston Villa player won the first ever Premier League goal of the season award?
  A. Dalian Atkinson
  B. David Platt
  C. Dwight Yorke

92. How many Aston Villa players have won the PFA Players' player of the year award?
  A. 1
  B. 2
  C. 3

93. How many Aston Villa players have won the PFA Young player of the year award?
  A. 3
  B. 4
  C. 5

94. Which of these famous actors is also an Aston Villa fan?
  A. Tom Cruise
  B. Tom Hanks
  C. Tom Hiddlestone

95. Which of these sports brands has not supplied kit to Aston Villa?
  A. Adidas
  B. Le Coq Sportif
  C. Umbro

96. How many players have scored for both Aston Villa and rivals Birmingham City in the Premier League?

A. 4

B. 5

C. 6

97. Which manager moved from Birmingham City to Aston Villa in 2011?

A. Paul Lambert

B. Brian Little

C. Alex McLeish

98. What is the club's official twitter account?

A. @AstonVilla

B. @AVFC

C. @AVFCOfficial

99. Tom Waring is the club's record goal scorer for a single season, but what was his nickname?

A. Bingo

B. Pongo

C. Tango

100. Who did Dion Dublin head-butt while playing for Aston Villa against Birmingham City?

A. Danny Murphy

B. Jason Roberts

C. Robbie Savage

101. Right here we go, the last question. Which Aston Villa manager waxed lyrical on the two M's: Movement and Positioning?

    A. Ron Atkinson

    B. John Gregory

    C. Martin O'Neill

Here are the answers to this block of questions.

A91. Villa legend Dalian Atkinson won the inaugural goal of the season competition in the first Premier League season back in 1992-93 with his stunning strike against Wimbledon.

A92. A total of three Aston Villa players have been voted Player of the year by their peers. They are Andy Gray, David Platt and Paul McGrath.

A93. Always a club with exciting young talent, four Villa players have been crowned Young player of the year. They are Andy Gray, Gary Shaw, Ashley Young and James Milner.

A94. Star of Toy Story, Castaway, The Terminal and Forrest Gump, actor Tom Hanks is also an Aston Villa supporter. Other famous fans include David Cameron and Prince William the Duke of Cambridge.

A95. Adidas has never supplied kit to Aston Villa. They are about the only manufacturer that hasn't!

A96. Several fans have risked the wrath of local fans by playing for both clubs, and six players have scored for both in the Premier League: Emile Heskey, Craig Gardner, Kevin Phillips, Dwight Yorke, Liam Ridgewell and Chris Sutton.

A97. Alex McLeish made the move across Birmingham to manage Villa days after his Blues side was relegated from the Premier League. He managed to anger fans of both clubs. Not a smart move, Alex.

A98. @AVFCOfficial is the club's official twitter account. It tweets multiple times daily and has over a million followers.

A99. Tom "Pongo" Waring once scored 50 goals in a season for Aston Villa between the wars. He was a born goal scorer, scoring 167 goals in 225 appearances. He even scored a hat trick on his debut. Where he got his nickname from though, no-one seems to know.

A100. Robbie Savage was on the wrong end of a Dion Dublin head-butt in the Second City Derby.

A101. This was just one of the many gaffes that escaped the mouth of "Big Ron" Atkinson, and there have been a few others we simply couldn't list in this family friendly quiz book.

That's it. That's a great question to finish with. I hope you enjoyed this book, and I hope you got most of the answers right.

I also hope you learnt some new facts about the club, and if you saw anything wrong, or have a general comment, please visit the glowwormpress.com website.

Thanks for reading, and if you did enjoy the book, would you be so kind as leave a positive review on Amazon.

Lightning Source UK Ltd.
Milton Keynes UK
UKHW040948191219
355624UK00030B/169/P